MW00915028

Copyright © 2017
All rights reserved

may not be reproduced or used in any manner whatsoever without the express written permission of the publisher except for the use of brief quotations in a book review.

Requests for permission to reproduce parts of this work should be addressed to the author. Contact information can be found on the author's website:

www.ordinarydudemeditation.com

If you would like to invite the author to speak at an event for your organization or are interested in his writing services, please contact him via the website.

TABLE OF CONTENTS

Introduction

Get ready to travel!

Greetings from Bangkok! I'm here to help you live the type of life I've been enjoying now for several years: one where you have the money and freedom to travel. Over the years there are a number of tricks I've learned to save money and cut corners on travel expenses. That's what this guide is about.

This guide is also here because I'm sure some of you reading this, and thinking about planning a trip abroad, are completely overwhelmed.

Maybe you're stuck in a minimum wage job, have lots of obligations, or are a generally busy person. You have no idea where to start planning or how to save money, so you just do nothing.

Well, that is exactly where I was at eight years ago in September 2010.

Since then, I have done two extended overseas excursions (totaling 5 years and counting) outside my home country. The first was an 11-month trip in 2010 and 2011 through Asia and Australia. The second was a more permanent move to Bangkok, Thailand where I currently reside as of December 2017.

During this time abroad, I've visited 12 different countries, two different continents, held six jobs making over $70,000 (Note: every time I use a $ sign I'm referring to US dollars) in the process, and been a tax paying citizen in both Thailand and Australia.

So how did I do this?

In this book, I am going to walk you through it.

But generally, the trick is to take everything one step at a time. Start with one small step, take another, keep doing it, and eventually you'll get there.

This guide includes tips to help you focus on each step, assist with your planning, and give you practical methods to save and make money.

Who this guide is for...

If you're planning on traveling to SE Asia or Australia and you're from the US, this guide will be invaluably helpful for you.

My tips are based off my travel experience. And since I'm from the US and traveled mostly through Australia and SE Asia, then everything in this guide will be applicable for you.

If you are not from the US or are traveling somewhere else, this guide can still be helpful. I've spoken with other travelers and researched other countries to find relevant info for your planning.

Some of the tips, especially my priority chapter (the most important chapter of the book) and frequent flyer mile chapter, can be applied to anyone anywhere.

5 tips to make your dream trip a reality

I've chosen to focus on five tips I believe can make the biggest difference in making your travel dreams a reality.

If I could go back in time and give myself a book to make getting abroad easier, the following pages are what I would have given. This is what I've learned that I wish I knew when I started.

The tips are broken up into chapters, and cover the following topics:

1. Frequent Flyer Miles (free airfare)
Shows beginners how to use FF miles to get free flights anywhere in the world.

2. Travel Vaccinations
Tips on how to get travel vaccinations for a much lower price than in the US.

3. Visas
How to prepare for Visas when traveling abroad.

4. Priorities
The most important chapter in the book. Tips on how to make your trip a priority so that you get out of the country and get abroad!

5. Australia
How to make a small fortune (I made $16,000 in five months in an unskilled job) while working and traveling in Australia.

For those interested in working abroad (and not just in Australia), I've included a bonus chapter, "How to find work abroad". This chapter goes into detail as to how I've scored six different jobs overseas.

This guide is intentionally short. The material is hyper-focused on practical tips to help make your dream trip a reality. In this updated version of the book (I released the original in 2014), I flirted with the idea of adding longer, personal stories to explain ideas.

After writing a test chapter, it simply wasn't working.

The longer stories were distracting from the beefy, practical tips that Backpack Abroad Now! is about.

The purpose of this book is to get you abroad. And I want to make that as simple, easy and clear as possible—getting right to the good stuff and to the point.

Now, let's get started!

Chapter 1

Mastering frequent flyer miles for beginners

Welcome to the world of free airfare!

In 2013 I booked two free flights using frequent flyer miles. The first was a round-trip flight from Chicago to Denver and the second was a one-way ticket from Chicago to Bangkok.

Since then, I also booked a free round trip ticket from Bangkok to Chicago in 2015, as well as few free domestic flights around that same time period.

Frequent flyer miles have saved me a ton of cash. In total, probably around $3,000 in airfare.

But before 2013, I had never used FF (frequent flyer) miles, nor knew much about them. In fact, I was actually scared of them! They seemed incredibly complicated, and I worried about all the credit cards I would have to apply for to accumulate miles.

But here's the secret.

FF miles are just a fancy pansy name for "award program" or "loyalty program". Have you ever signed up for one?

Back in the states I was a member of Best Buy's and Firestone's reward programs. So if you're a member of these or any others—like Starbucks, Panera Bread, Regal Cinemas, etc.—then you already have some experience with this type of thing.

FF Miles work in a similar way to any award program. They just have a fancier, scarier name that is associated with the high cost item known as airfare. And I assure you, they're not as frightening or difficult as you may think. Anyone can learn this.

Strategy to gain miles

There are several ways you can gain frequent flyer miles: with credit cards, signing up for FF programs (which you'll have to do eventually), or joining a program like Chris Guillebeau's Travel Hacking Cartel: travelhacking.org

Recommended FF Programs

Two programs I like are:

1. ***United MileagePlus:***
   a. Recommended card: MileagePlus Explorer

2. ***American Airlines AA Advantage:***
   a. Recommended card: AAdvantage Platinum Select

Whatever airline you sign up with, they all work in a similar fashion. The mileage program/airline will send you e-mails about deals to get miles: by eating at certain restaurants, using specific services like internet or cable providers, opening a particular bank account, test driving cars, etc.

Once you've signed up for a FF Program, you will also gain miles when you fly with that airline. The catch is, you will need to book the flight through your airline's website.

To find a FF Program, just Google *[name of airline] frequent flyer program*, click on the link, and sign up from there. Easy as pie.

Travel Hacking Cartel

I have yet to try Guillebeau's service. But judging from the website, it looks like it includes an orientation to the world of free airfare as well as tips on the best deals to gain miles right now. Check it out here: travelhacking.org

Why am I recommending a product I don't use? Because I trust Guillebeau. His book (which I introduce later in this chapter) helped ease me into the world of FF Miles and made all my free flights possible.

The main reason I'm not a Travel Hacking Cartel member today is because I live in Bangkok and, from my understanding, his program caters mostly to US residents. But you can be sure, the moment I move permanently back to the US I'll be a proud member.

Brief Tangent: Can you score hordes of FF Miles if you live outside the US?

Good question. From traveling all over Asia and Australia I have learned a few significant differentiators between US and foreign airlines.

1. In terms of service and quality, US flights are well below the standard of other first world airlines. Frankly, US airlines suck.
2. US FF Mile programs reign supreme over foreign counterparts.

Personally, I will take an awesome FF program compared to great in-flight service any day. When it comes to flying, the destination is the goal—not the journey.

So if you live in the US, congratulations! You have access to the best FF Mile programs in the world. Feel free to skip ahead to *The "Rack Up Miles" Credit Card Philosophy* section, as the rest of this part is written specifically for non-US residents.

For everyone else, there is still hope…

Australia has some decent programs. This nifty site lists some great credit cards to accumulate miles quickly: finder.com.au/best-frequent-flyer-program
- Google *best frequent flyer program finder**

A few notable Australian cards to check out include:
- Virgin Australia Velocity Flyer
- ANZ Frequent Flyer Black

For Brits, this article is a good starting point: thepointsguy.com/2014/10/top-uk-credit-cards-british-airways-hilton-and-more/
- Google *the points guy top UK credit cards*

A few notable UK cards:
- British Airways American Express Cards
- Virgin Atlantic Black

As for those of you in Asian countries…well, the programs here suck. The Thai airways Royal Orchid Plus program is a complete joke. My girlfriend has spent over $15,000 US dollars on the card in three years and has still yet to receive a free flight, as miles are devalued several times annually.

As links don't work in the hard copy of this book, I've added keywords (in italics) here to help you search the article in Google. Every time you see a crazy looking url, I'll use this same style to help you find the resource.

If you want to use credit cards here, it's best to sign up for a program in a first world country and then use the credit card in Asia, South America or wherever you may be. Many US cards can be used abroad with no foreign transaction fees.

The catch is you will need a foreign bank account. If you are a westerner living in Asia, you can still apply for credit cards in your home country. I did this in 2015 to score my biggest bonus ever – 50,000 miles – for just making a single purchase on the card.

The "Rack Up Miles" Credit Card Philosophy

Generally, there are two ways to rack up miles quickly with Credit Cards.

Strategy 1: Go after the big spend bonuses.

You get the big miles bonuses after spending a certain amount of money on the card within a time frame. This amount of money is known as the "minimum spend".

For example, on my "Citi Platinum Select AA Advantage World MasterCard," I had to spend $1000 (the minimum spend) on the card within 3 months to earn the 30,000 mile bonus.

Credit Card bonuses are usually anywhere from 25,000 to 50,000 miles. And to get it you have to spend amounts from $500 to $5000 within a month to year time range. Also, you usually get a mile or two for every dollar you spend on the card.

Strategy 2: Sign up for cards with "single-purchase only" bonuses

Sometimes cards require no amount of spending. You just get a bonus for your first purchase. For example, back in 2013 I was able to score 10,000 bonus miles after my first purchase using American Express's "Starwood Preferred Guest Card". Starwood has since wised up, and this deal is no longer available.

With that said, these deals do come along every now and then. You just need to keep your ears open.

As mentioned earlier, I scored 50,000 miles in 2015 after signing up for the US Airways Dividends Miles MasterCard and making just a single purchase.

This deal was only available because US Airways was being bought by American Airlines, and the credit card was being discontinued. Luckily I got news of this deal from Chris Guillebeau via his Unconventional Guides newsletter.

How can you catch wind of "single-purchase only" Credit Card deals?

I was automatically signed up to Chris's newsletter because I bought his Frequent Flyer Master book. As of this writing I have yet to find a way to sign up for this list without buying the book.

But not to fear.

There are dozens of frequent flyer websites online that are almost certain to alert you to new deals. This article by the Penny Hoarder lists some of the best sites: thepennyhoarder.com/smart-money/travel-hacking-blogs/
- Google *penny hoarder 21 travel hacks*

Alternatively, Credit Cards for Travel is always on top of the latest CC news and the site lists some of the best bonuses on offer. At the bottom of their page—cardsfortravel.com/getting-started—you can sign up for their newsletter to get alerts for the best deals of the moment.
- Google *cards for travel started*

My Strategy for getting a free flight from Chicago to Bangkok

I simply used credit cards, and here's what I did. Using Guillebeau's *Frequent Flyer Master* book frequentflyermaster.com and doing my own research, I chose the cards with the biggest bonuses that would take the least effort to gain miles.

On the next page, was my strategy.

Card	Minimum Spend	Spending Time Frame	Bonus Miles
Delta Skymiles Card	$500	3 months	30,000
American Express Starwood Card	Bonus upon first purchase	none	10,000
Citibank AA Advantage Visa	$1000	3 months	30,000
Citibank AA Advantage MasterCard	$1000	3 months	30,000

Note: Some of these bonuses in the chart above have changed since I used them. As mentioned, the Starwood deal is long gone. And all "Delta Skymiles Card" now requires a $1000 minimum spend.

I will address how to overcome the spend bonuses of today's credit cards, but first I want to give you a better understanding of how to use a system to accumulate miles.

How to not lose money with Credit Cards

Many people have problems with credit cards, racking up tons of debt and buying things they can't afford. That's not what we're about here.

Instead, we're going to use a system that ensures we rack up the most bonuses /miles without it ever costing us a dime.

When I was using credit cards to gain miles in 2013, I created a Word doc listing all my cards so I could keep myself on track. On the following page is the system I used to monitor my credit cards. For simplicity purposes, I only include three of my eight cards on this list.

CREDIT CARD TRACKING

AIRFARE CARDS

CITIBANK MASTERCARD
ACTIVE BALANCE
Number of dollars spent needed to hit bonus: 1000
Bonus Goal Date: July 15
Date needed to cancel card by: March 2014
        Approved on: April 22, 2013
Payment Amount: 627
Payment Due Date: 6th of the month
APR: 17.24%

DELTA AMEX SKYMILES
INACTIVE
Number of dollars spent needed to hit bonus: 500
Bonus Goal Date: COMPLETED
Date needed to cancel card by: March 2014
        Approved on: April 22, 2013
Payment Amount: none
Payment Due Date: 27th of month
APR:

OTHER CARDS

BEST BUY CARD
Balance: $0
Payment Due Date: 20th of the month

APR: 13.24%
Notes: Should probably cancel this card. I have no intention of using it anytime soon.

Break down of above information

If you need a more detailed explanation of the above list, on the next page is a breakdown of what I did, with more information. Otherwise, feel free to skip this section.

Name of the Credit Card

Is your card ACTIVE or INACTIVE?
Are you using it? Is there a balance for this month?

Number of dollars spent needed to hit bonus:
How much money you need to spend on the card to
get the bonus.

Bonus Goal Date:
What date do you want to reach the bonus by?

Date needed to cancel card by:
Most cards have an annual fee that is waived the
first year. If you don't cancel the card by a certain
date, you'll be charged this fee. It's good to note this
date so you don't forget to cancel the card (unless
you want to pay the annual fee and keep it).

Approved on:
The date your card was approved.

Payment Amount:
How much money I have on the card for this
month's billing period.

Payment Due Date:
Date I need to pay my bill by.

APR:
Not necessary, but I included it for some of my
cards.

Template for your use

If you want to use this method for keeping track of your cards, the template is below. Just fill in the appropriate information for each card you have.

Name of card here
ACTIVE or INACTIVE
Number of dollars spent needed to hit bonus:
Bonus Goal Date:
Date needed to cancel card by:
        Approved on:
Payment Amount:
Payment Due Date:
APR:

The need for a system

With numerous cards (especially when you have eight like I did), some kind of tracking system is necessary. A single slip up and you could be paying interest and not getting your trip for free.

As an additional tip…if you choose to sign up for several cards, I highly recommend prioritizing your credit cards as one of the most important things you focus on.

One of the most common reasons people get into trouble with credit cards is they aren't paying attention to their spending. To overcome this, you just need to prioritize the monitoring of your cards. I explain more about prioritization in Chapter 4, so simply apply the techniques I mention in that chapter: dedicate time every week to monitoring your cards.

How to hit credit card minimum spends

I know what you're thinking. How the heck do you hit the minimum spend on these cards to get the bonuses?

With spend limits ranging anywhere from $1,000 - $5000 in a three month time frame, it can be a bit mind boggling…especially if you're broke.

The key is to plan your most expensive purchases to occur within a small window. I did this in 2013 by waiting to pay my next 6 months of health insurance, 6 months of car insurance, new website, and major car repairs all within a three month period.

I knew these purchases were necessary, so I decided to see if it was possible to just pay them all on credit cards within a few month period. So I called up my car and health insurance providers and asked if I could pay the next 6 months premiums early.

Of course, they were happy to take my money.

And because I was able to score huge mile bonuses, I was more than thrilled to give it to them.

Okay John, that was back in 2013...how can you hit minimum spends in 2018?

You're right. Times have changed in the frequent flyer mile world. For the most part, $500, $1,000 spend bonuses and free sign-up bonuses have disappeared...for the most part.

So I want to show you how you can still accumulate miles today.

In April of 2018, I plan to make a one-month trip back to the US. And as I have to make a lot of purchases during this time, I will sign up for a few credit cards to rack up miles. Here's what I intend to do:

Sign up for
- 1 Citibank AAdvantage card
- 1 Barclay Arrival Plus card

Total minimum spend: $4,000
Time frame: 3 months
Total miles: 80,000

To reach the $4,000 minimum spend, the first thing I want to do is map out all the fixed expenses I have in the time frame between April 1 and April 31, 2018. Based on my past experiences and purchase history, here are the estimated minimum amounts I will spend on each item.

Fixed expenses

- Round-trip ticket from Bangkok to Chicago $1,000
- Computer $1,200
- A month's worth of expenses back home*: $1,200
- Renew websites: $250
- Renew domains: $115

Total: $3,765

The month's worth of expenses will be spent on food, domestic flights, gifts, Amazon orders, entertainment, etc.

That leaves me $235 short of the minimum spend. So I need a backup plan to account for this cash. Here are a couple options I'm considering...

- Pay a year of health ins. premiums upfront: $776
- Sign up for an online course: $300
- Buy advertising for this or another book: $235 worth
- Book flights for upcoming trips: $235 worth

As I'm in Thailand, I'm not entirely sure if my provider will let me pay a year's worth of my health insurance premiums upfront. But it is something I will surely try if I need to hit the minimum spend. If that doesn't work, I'll likely consider spending that money on another typical expense of mine—online courses, which I typically spend around $500 a year on.

Worse comes to worse, I will just spend the money on book advertising or future flights as I regularly spend money on both these expenses.

As for you, there is one major fixed expense I have left off this list: rent.

Yes, you can actually pay for rent with a credit card, even if your landlord doesn't accept credit card payments. A few services that can help you do this are below:

- plastiq.com
- onradpad.com

When I move permanently back to the US, I will certainly be using these services to rack up some fat bonuses for credit card spending. I highly advise you to do the same if your trying to reach the minimum spend quickly.

So the point of all this...

I just want show you how it is possible to plan expenses in advance to hit minimum spends. All you have to do is think ahead. And you can almost certainly get some big bonus miles to land your dream travel excursion, while simply spending money you were going to spend anyway.

Is there an easier way?

There might be. What I shared above is actually my second option. But I wanted to show you a more challenging scenario first, so you can see how hitting a higher minimum spend is possible.

So what's my first option?

From my research, it appears that you can sign up for a Citibank AAdvantage personal card and Citibank AAdvantage business card at the same time – effectively qualifying for the 30,000 mile bonus on both cards.

If my research is correct, that means you can get 60,000 miles for a low $2,000 minimum spend in 3 months. Pretty nice, huh?

So my original plan will be this:

Sign up for
- 1 Citibank AAdvantage personal card
- 1 Citibank AAdvantage business card

Total minimum spend: $2,000
Total Miles: 60,000

What about your credit score?

The truth is, you may lose a few points. When signing up for multiple cards at the same time it's gonna happen. But your score will go back up. A few weeks after I signed up for four FF credit cards, my score was still in the high 700's.

Also, remember—credit cards have annual fees

If you didn't notice, generally FF credit cards have annual fees. So if you sign up for four of them and don't want to pay the fees, remember to cancel them by the time your year is up. The fees can be quite pricey, ranging from $50 to $500.

Still scared of credit cards and FF miles?

It's okay. We are all human. Just remember that with nearly any new experience or activity you try, there is always a bit of fear.

Think back to your first experience swimming, riding a bike or going to high school. All of them were likely scary at first. But the more you did those activities the more you became comfortable with them. Then one day the fear disappeared completely. It's the same thing with credit cards and frequent flyer miles.

If you're still scared, I would recommend educating yourself a bit more before getting started.

I again recommend Guillebeau's *Frequent Flyer Master* book frequentflyermaster.com *as he* gives you a very thorough orientation to the process, and it was a huge help for myself.

A few other frequent flyer resources worth checking out include:
- millionmilesecrets.com

- thepointsguy.com
- flyertalk.com

Chapter 2

How to save BIG on travel vaccinations

If you live in the US, travel vaccinations can cost you a small fortune. Before I departed on my 11-month journey in 2010, I spent about $1,800 on a series of six different travel vaccines.

Realize that travel vaccinations can cost much less outside your home country, especially if you're from the US.

When I arrived in Bangkok in September 2013, I updated my vaccinations here for a fraction of what it would have cost in the US. I got my Japanese Encephalitis and Typhoid shots for around $30 here. Whereas those same shots would have cost me over $600 in the states.

It's not just those two shots that cost less. If I had gotten my entire shot sequence from my first trip abroad while in Bangkok (the six that cost me $1,800), I would have spent less than $150. Rabies alone cost me $900 in the US, but less that $45 in Bangkok.

Other medical treatment overseas

I recently went to the dentist for a cleaning here in Bangkok this past January. Smile Bangkok Dentists did an excellent job on my teeth and again cost me a fraction of what it would have in the US—$30 as opposed to the almost $200 cleaning in the states.

I've also been doing some natural treatment for hair loss here that has worked gangbusters. The cost is only $15 a month.

Is it safe to get medical treatment overseas?

Yes and no. My mother is endlessly worried about this, but if you do your research there is nothing to worry about. Millions of foreigners get medical treatment in Bangkok every year.

Just make sure the medical facilities you visit, properly sterilize their instruments and use new needles, wear gloves, etc.

There are plenty of clinics that do none of this in third world countries, and there are plenty that do. Unfortunately most people focus on the bad ones, making a big huff and puff about it completely ignoring the ones that follow hygienic and safe practices.

Of course I could have gone to the dentist for $11, but maybe it would have been questionable as to whether or not they were using the proper and safe instruments. I chose to spend a bit more ($30, which is a lot in Thailand) and found a reputable company that I knew was going to be safe.

Can you find inexpensive vaccinations if you're traveling outside of Asia?

Yes. But…I just want to be clear; I am not a health care professional.

The advice I give is based off my own experience getting vaccinations here in Bangkok and research on vaccination clinics in South America and Africa—two continents I've never visited.

If you choose to get vaccinations outside of your home country, you do so at your own risk. So **do some research on the clinic before getting vaccinated there**. Check out their website, or better yet, just give them a call. You can do this pretty easily, and affordably, with Skype.

With that said, I recommend checking out the Thai Red Cross in Bangkok as I've gotten my own vaccines there.

So what about South America and Africa?

For South Africa, I found this clinic, which looks to be reasonably affordable…traveldoctor.co.za/price-list-johannesburg
- Google *travel doctor johannesburg price list*

As for South America…I couldn't find any clinic's vaccine pricing list, but I've read numerous reports that free or low cost (as in under $50) Rabies and

Yellow Fever vaccines are offered in some places throughout the continent.

The point of all this is, I want you to know that even outside of Asia, cheap vaccinations (far below the outrageous costs in the US) are possible.

If you're traveling to Europe or Australia (I didn't get any for Australia), travel vaccinations are less of an issue since you'll likely not need many vaccinations to go there. Regardless, I still advise checking the recommended vaccinations of the specific country your going to.

You can find out what vaccines you need here: cdc.gov/travel, and you can also make an appointment at a travel clinic to talk with a doctor about what vaccines you need. While I consulted with a doctor before both my trips, I have friends who skipped this step.

The choice is entirely up to you.

If you live in the US where vaccines are ridiculously expensive, it's worth considering getting them abroad where it's much more inexpensive. A Travel doctor I visited in the US even told me that US vaccines are overpriced and recommended I get them outside the country.

Chapter 3

Making sense of visas
For short & extended trips

Before I set out on my 11 month backpacking journey, I was pretty confused about visas. I knew I'd be travelling to at least eight or nine countries, so how was I supposed to go about getting them?

Should I apply for all of them in advance? When I do apply, is it difficult to get the visa? How expensive will they be?

In this chapter, I intend to fill you in on how to go about securing visas. And it is much easier than you may think. I'll give you a basic idea of visa requirements in particular regions, as well as general principles to keep in mind when applying.

Let's start off with some guidelines first.

Should you apply for visas before you leave your home country?

It depends. To find this out, you first need to answer two questions:

1. Do you need to apply for a visa at all?
2. How many countries will you visit?

Question 1: Depending on what countries you're traveling to, your nationality and how long you're traveling, you may not need any visas at all. For example, let's say you're an American traveling to Thailand, South Africa and Singapore. Your trip is for one month, and you won't stay longer than 15 days in any country.

Guess what? You won't be spending a dime on visas.

As of December 2017, Americans (and many western country nationalities) can enter Thailand, Singapore and South Africa without a visa—for anywhere between 15 and 90 days.

Pretty cool, huh?

In addition to countries where applying for a visa is completely unnecessary, there are also many countries that offer another service that makes applying for visas incredibly easy: visa on arrival.

What's a visa on arrival?

Well, exactly what it sounds like. Once you arrive at the airport or get to the land border, you can apply for the visa right then and there. Yes, they are as awesome as they sound.

I've personally gotten visas on arrival several times. For example, in Indonesia I applied for my visa at a booth in Jakarta's airport before I passed through immigration. In Laos and Cambodia, I did the same thing at the land border before I crossed over.

Obtaining your visa on arrival is a quick and cheap process. Generally it'll be issued within 5 to 30 minutes, and it will cost less than $50 bucks. Even better, you typically get a nice shiny sticker in your passport as opposed to just a stamp.

Here's my visa on arrival from a previous Laos border crossing.

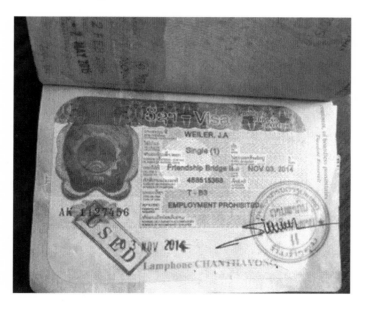

Looks pretty cool if you ask me.

To know if you qualify for a visa on arrival, simply Google the visa requirements of whatever country you're traveling to.

Question 2: In many cases, when you're visiting multiple countries you'll need to get at least one visa.

If the first country you're visiting requires a visa (and you can't obtain it upon arrival) then you'll need to apply in advance. And if you're visiting multiple countries within a short time period, and all of them require visas, then it's wise to apply for all visas before your trip.

Applying for a visa in your home country is relatively easy. If you live in or near a big city, you can go to your local embassy and apply. Otherwise you'll have to apply for the visa by mail.

One special note...while it's good to apply for the visa as far in advance as possible, make sure you know how long the visa is valid.

For instance, when I applied for my China visa in August of 2011, I was required to enter the country before November 24 of that year. If I had tried to enter past that date, I would've been rejected – as the visa would've been expired.

The point is, don't apply too early. Or else the visa may expire before you even enter the country.

To sum all this up, check visa requirements beforehand to know whether you even need a visa for a country or you can get one on arrival. And if you do apply before you trip, remember not to do so too early.

How to find a country's visa requirements in under 5 minutes

If you've ever applied for a visa before, you can probably skip this section, as you likely already know how to find visa requirements. But for those of you who've never travelled abroad (or for Americans who have only visited Canada and Mexico – which was me before I backpacked for 11 months), then you may be a bit unsure how to find your visa requirements.

I'm going to break it down for you very easily here.

It all comes down to simply Googling the requirements of the country you're planning to visit.

Step 1: Google *[name of desired country] visa requirements [your nationality]*.

Step 2: Click on the link of your government's official website for visas. This can usually be identified by the .gov domain extension or .gc (for Canada). It's important you visit your government's website, because otherwise you may go to a visa agency service that could provide incorrect information.

Step 3: Read the visa requirements for the country.

Step 4: Google *[country you're visiting] embassies in [your home country].* This will return locations of your desired destination's embassies. If an embassy is located in a nearby city, you can go and apply for the visa in person. If not, you can apply by mail.

Step 5: Call the embassy you wish to apply. I recommend doing this beforehand just so you can double-check your visa requirements.

Once you do this, you can simply visit the embassy to apply for the visa, or mail in your pictures and paperwork. Easy as pie.

For Americans, Canadians and UK citizens…if you want to skip step one, here are the government websites for you to check visa requirements:

- Americans: travel.state.gov/content/passports/en/passports.html
- Canadians: canada.ca/en.html
- UK Citizens: gov.uk/foreign-travel-advice

Handling visas when travelling for extended periods

In cases where you are travelling for periods of 3 months or longer, the best way to get visas is to simply apply for them as you go.

If the first country you're visiting requires a visa, I recommend applying for this before leaving home. Afterwards, you can simply apply for visas on the fly.

For example, say you started your trip in the Philippines. You've been there a few weeks and now you're ready to move on to your next destination. Simply Google the visa requirements online of wherever you're traveling to next. You may learn you don't need a visa, you can get a visa on arrival or you need to apply for a visa in advance.

If you need to apply in advance, you can either apply in person at an embassy in the Philippines, or you may be able to visit a local travel agency that will handle the visa application for you. Either way is fine, and local travel agencies are prevalent in backpacker and tourist areas.

With that said, if you do use a local travel agency, make sure they are legitimate.

Yes, it's true local agencies typically cost more than applying in person, but sometimes agencies will overcharge you excessively. In other words, they're ripping you off. So it's wise to get some feedback on the travel agency instead of just blindly showing up and trusting them with your money and visa. Especially since some agencies may actually provide you a fake visa, which could get you in a lot of trouble further down the line.

You can find out if a local travel agency has a good reputation by doing one of three things:

1. Google the travel agencies name online and read the comments about them by other travelers
2. Ask other travelers you meet about the agency
3. Ask your guesthouse or hotel about legitimate agencies to use

As a traveler, people will almost always try and scam you. But if you follow the three steps above, the chances of you getting a fake visa or getting ripped off are incredibly slim—to the point it's not worth worrying about.

The reason I bring all this scamming talk up?

Backpackers typically stand out in foreign countries. And if your skin color does not match that of the country's majority population, then you are an obvious target.

Brief Tangent: How a Google "Scams" search can save you $1,400

No joke. I was scammed for $1,400 in Cambodia at the tail end of my 11-month backpacking trip. But if I had followed the simple tip I'm about to share with you, I would've avoided it.

Though scams are not the focus of this book…as a fellow traveler, I want you to avoid mistakes myself and others have made. So here's what I recommend doing in the weeks before boarding your flight.

Google one or both of the following:
- *[name of country you're visiting] scams*
- *[name of country you're visiting] top 10 scams*

Doing this, will bring up all the common scams tourists are often duped for. Some of them are downright frightening, and others may cost you less than $20.

But if you're anything like me, even being ripped off just $5 can ruin your day. Often the amount of money you lose doesn't matter. It's the principle and fact you're being cheated that causes hours of anger and frustration.

So what scam cost me $1,400 cash?

This one: phnompenhpost.com/national/blackjack-scam-bust-tourists
- Google *blackjack scam tourist bust*

And had I followed the guidelines above, it would've never happened.

So please do yourself a favor and Google scams of your destination. This simple tip could be worth a thousand times the cost of this book alone.

Visa rules and regulations change regularly

Before getting into some of the details of different region's visa applications, it's important to know that visa rules and regulations change all the time. The below guidelines are what is true as of writing in December 2017.

While I don't expect much of the following general guidelines to change within the next 5 years, I highly recommended researching your unique visa requirements before your trip.

Regional visa overviews

Southeast Asia

Visas in Southeast Asia are no problem. In most countries you'll be visa exempt or can apply for a visa on arrival, which is good for anywhere from 15 to 90 days. This is basically just a stamp or sticker you get in your passport at the airport/border crossing of your destination. Costs typically range from free to $50.

South America

The most notable thing about South American visas is, they are expensive (at least for Americans). Visa fees for countries such as Venezuela, Bolivia and Brazil are all over $100.

Africa

To my delightful surprise, my research has shown that many African visas are incredibly convenient or free. Popular countries such as South Africa, Namibia and Morocco require no visa at all for Americans. And other countries—such as Tanzania, Egypt and Kenya—offer visas on arrival for a reasonable fee (under $50).

Europe

If only more regions offered the amazing **European Power visa** (not its actual name). This visa, called the Schengen visa, provides travelers access to 25 European countries with one (you heard that right, ONE) reasonably priced visa. As this is a budget travel book, I imagine most of you reading this will not be going to Europe because of the higher cost. But you'll at least be happy to know if you do, you'll be saving money on visas.

Wherever you're traveling, the trick with visas is to not overwhelm yourself.

If you're planning a 3-month (or longer) trip, worry only about the first one. Once you are abroad and preparing to move to your next country, then start researching your next visa.

How long does it take to get your visa after applying?

Most embassies can turn it around in just a couple days, sometimes only a single day. With that said, if you apply by mail it will obviously take longer.

Also, when applying at embassies in person (whether at home or in a foreign country) it's wise to be aware of the embassy's holidays. Usually an embassy will be closed on the holidays of both their native country and the country they're located in.

For example, a Thai embassy in Malaysia will generally be closed on Malaysian national holidays and Thai national holidays.

In other words, it's wise to check the embassy's holiday schedule (usually found on their website) before applying. Otherwise it may be closed the day you plan to apply, or the day after. Both cases will cause a delay in getting your visa.

A special note on your departing flight from your home country

I'm not sure if this is the same in Europe and Australia, but US airlines require a round-trip ticket or onward flight for international travel. What that means is you can't fly to Thailand, Ireland, Argentina, etc. on a one-way ticket. Both times I've flown one-way internationally from the US, I was asked for my onward ticket.

If you are asked and don't have one, you won't be allowed on the flight. If you find yourself in this situation, I would recommend buying a fully refundable ticket or the cheapest one you can find. I've heard from travelers who've been in this predicament, that they bought a ticket on their smartphone and showed the airlines the electronic copy via their phone. If you don't have a smartphone, you should be able to buy a ticket physically at the airport.

I've also heard of this happening outside of the US. For example, I met a traveler who was flying one-way from Indonesia to Malaysia and was asked for her onward ticket. She didn't have it and had to do the smartphone trick.

The likelihood of this happening to you is uncertain. Outside the US, I've never had anyone ask me about my onward ticket (and I bought a lot of one-way tickets). But I'd rather be prepared than be in a last minute jam at the airport.

Getting around the onward ticket requirement

If you are planning an open-ended trip like I did, then there are a few different strategies to solve this problem.

I have bought a "junk ticket" every time. That means I buy the absolutely cheapest international ticket I can find to show the Airline Attendant. Highest I've ever spent is around $40, lowest is in the $20 range. To find these low international fairs, research what the budget airlines are in the region you're traveling to. Then find the shortest distance, one-way international booking.

Another option is to buy a fully refundable ticket. They are generally hundreds of dollars more expensive than regular flights. I've been too scared to try them for fear of misreading some detail in the fine print that would cause me to lose the entire fair. It's not worth the risk or effort for me, so I get the junk ticket. But there are plenty of travelers who opt for the refundable one.

Chapter 4

How to set priorities To guarantee you travel abroad

More than anything, if you want to travel or live abroad you need to make it a **priority**.

This is the key to everything and most important tip in this book.

If you don't follow this guideline, you will inevitably fail (unless you win the lotto or already have the money saved). That means most of your energy and attention should be going to making your travel goal happen. Spend at least an hour a day, five days a week, working on making your trip a reality.

How to spend this time

Research...
- Where you are going to go.
- Costs of where you are going, costs of activities there, how you'll get around, and where you'll stay.
- How you can cut your current expenses to save money.
- FF miles.

Also, think about...

- Coming up with a budget.
- Savings goals you can set for each month.

What is a savings goal?

Exactly what it sounds like: a specific amount of money you are trying to save. Typically, I would always break my savings goal down by month.

For example, while I was saving to move to Thailand in 2013, my monthly savings goal varied from month to month, but on average was five hundred dollars a month.

If you aren't making a lot of money and want to travel, a savings goal is a helpful solution to keep you on track putting money aside.

Cutting expenses

Before my first extended trip overseas in 2010, I lived in a dining room for a year at a rent of $200 a month. During this time, I set aside money every month for travel savings (savings goal), all the while taking time to research where I'd stay, countries I'd visit, activities I'd do, and the costs of all this.

Maybe you don't need to go to the extreme of living in a dining room, but picking up roommates or downsizing your apartment can also help. Rent is a big expense, and finding a way to chop this down can quickly save you a lot of money for your travel dream.

Of course there are other ways: going out less, drinking alcohol less or cutting out alcohol all together, and selling you car (you won't be needing it anyways if you're going to be spending over a year abroad. I sold mine the month before I left for Bangkok back in 2013, and to this day I still think it was a great decision).

Also, watching what you eat is a great way to save money.

Eat out less, and start eating more foods you can buy in bulk for a cheap price. A Costco card is obviously a great idea. But even without a Costco card, you can still buy rice, beans, and oatmeal very cheaply, and these can make up a good deal of your meals.

I'm not saying live like a monk and only eat plain rice, beans, or oatmeal. There are easy ways to spice these dishes up by adding sauces, spices, bulk meat, and frozen veggies (also in bulk at Costco).

Not to mention eating rice and oatmeal is good for your health, and you may even end up shedding some pounds depending on your normal diet.

Other options

- Work harder to make more money.
- Move in with your parents.

For my move to Thailand in 2013, I moved in with my parents because failure wasn't an option. If I failed, then my relationship with my girlfriend (who's from Bangkok) probably would have as well.

While living with my parents for ten months, I paid off $1,500 in debt, over $2,000 in car repairs, and saved $3,600 towards moving abroad. And I was only working for seven of those months.

Living with parents can be demoralizing for some. But if travel is something that is a **priority** and you can't afford to fail, then put your ego in check and do it. You'll soon forget it when you're living your dream abroad.

Focusing on the Big Wins

In Ramit Sethi's book, "I Will Teach You to be Rich," he writes about focusing on your big wins.

This advice was invaluable to me while saving for my move to Bangkok.

What are Big Wins?

Big wins are the things that give you the greatest pleasure for your money.

Is that food? Socializing with friends? Partying?

We all have activities that give us greater pleasure than others. Figure out what yours are, prioritize them, and then cut back on other expenses.

Your Big Wins

Obviously travel is a big win for you. That's why you're saving. But what are your big wins that will bring you happiness while you're saving?

For me, it was eating out and basketball. In the months leading to my move abroad, I went to four NBA games and ate out once a week.

Doing this gave me great pleasure and helped make my life enjoyable while I was cutting back on things not as important to me: partying, going out for drinks and socializing with friends on a weekly basis, buying new clothes and electronics, etc.

Choose one or two big wins. Put aside a couple hundred dollars towards them a month, and it will go a long way to increasing your happiness while saving for your trip.

Start today

Whatever you plan to do, get started on it immediately. If you keep thinking and telling people about how you want to travel but do nothing, nothing will happen. So get going!

Chapter 5

AUSTRALIA...

The gold mine many Americans have never heard of

Ever hear of the Work and Holiday visa? It allows you to work and travel in Australia while making oodles of money on your adventure abroad. I made $16,000 within five months of being in Australia, and I only worked three and a half of those months.

Work and Holiday visa or Working Holiday visa?

It's confusing, but these are actually two different visas that essentially do the same thing: allow foreigners to work and travel in Oz (Australia).

The difference? It all comes down to nationality. Americans apply for one, Germans the other, etc.

Depending on your nationality, you may even be able to apply online like I did.

For more details, check out Australia's immigration website:

Visa for Americans: border.gov.au/Trav/Visa-1/462-
- Google *Australia holiday visa 462*

Visa for other nationalities: border.gov.au/Trav/Visa-1/417-

- Google *Australia holiday visa 417*

The $5,000 sufficient fund requirement

It should be noted, when applying for the Australian Work and Holiday visa, not all of the requirements are taken very seriously.

As this is a book for budget travelers, I specifically want to address the "AU $5,000 evidence of sufficient funds requirement". This supposedly requires a copy of your bank statement showing you have access to this much money.

Back in 2011, this requirement still existed. And I was just as scared of it as you may be. So I asked other travelers who had gotten the visa how they got around this requirement. The answer is, that none of them were ever asked to prove this. And neither was I when I was there.

To this day, it still looks that this requirement is rarely if ever enforced. A report from Girlunmapped.com suggests this is still the case today.*

If you are still worried about this requirement, it's probably worth doing some sleuthing to see what other travelers experience is with this. My guess is that it is still a non-issue, but a bit of research and asking around can help calm your nerves if you're worried about not getting accepted for the visa.

*_girlunmapped.com/work-and-holiday-visa-australia_ is the page that reports the $5,000 visa requirement still is likely a non-issue. This page is also worth checking out to get further info about this visa.

- Google _girl unmapped work and holiday_

Growing a small fortune in Oz

Though not as easy as it used to be, making a lot of money quickly is still possible in Australia.

When I was there in 2011, the US and Ozzie dollar had the same exchange rate, meaning one US dollar was worth one Australian dollar. Since then, that's changed.

But at the time of this writing in December 2017, for every one Australian dollar you make, you get the equivalent of .81 cents. And considering the minimum wage in Australia is over AUD $18 an hour (the equivalent of nearly $15 USD), you can still bank with a job or two in Oz.

Best of all, jobs are easy to come by, especially if you have few expectations for where you want to work. Again, this comes down to priority. If you want to make tons of money in Oz, you will. You just have to be willing to work in the sticks and possibly not have your dream job, location, or hours.

Lucky for me, I got everything I was looking for: an easy job, paying $21 an hour in a small country town that embodied the laid back Ozzie lifestyle. I won't lie, I worked lots of hours (even broke my record for number of days worked in a row—somewhere over 30), but money was my priority so it didn't matter.

How I found this goldmine of a job

I simply opened my mouth. It always amazes me how the simple act of speaking up and advertising what you want can land you what you're looking for.

Hostels are a great place to "network." I told other travelers what I was looking for, and one day a young German guy named Bjorn gave me a lead on my dream job (thank you Bjorn wherever you are!).

Bjorn had just been working in the countryside making bank, and he gave me a contact for the caravan (trailer) park he'd been staying at. I called the park owner, and she hooked me up with a job. Boom!

The trailer park was great! I know many people conjure up images of hillbillies in wife beaters when they think of trailer parks, but it was none of this. Over the course of my 11-month trip, it was the nicest place I stayed. And there were even other backpackers staying there I made friends with.

My trailer's kitchen…small, but delightful

Bed to the right, bathroom behind the door to the left, extra sleeping quarters (that I never used) in the back

The lovely exterior

How much money should you have saved to go to Oz on this magical visa?

I had about $1,300 and got my first paycheck when I had roughly $400 left. Took me two weeks to find my job upon arrival.

However, I'd recommend having at least $3,000 if you're going to just show up in Oz. With the extra money to survive on, you'll feel less stress during your job search. It also buys you more time to consider different job options. But as you can see from me, it can be done for less.

Lining up jobs beforehand while outside of Australia

From all I've heard, and through personal experience, I've heard it's quite difficult.

Employers actually want to see you there ready and willing to work before they hire you. If you think about it, why would they choose someone abroad when they already have plenty of workers to choose from right in front of them?

Despite this, I've spoken with other travelers who've successfully used agencies to line up work before arrival in Oz. So it is possible to do this.

An alternative solution—Travelers At Work

A month before I headed to Oz in 2011, I joined TAW (travelers at work) in an attempt to line up work. I applied for a dozen or so jobs and only heard back from one.

Again, my disadvantage was that I wasn't physically in Australia. Maybe things have changed since then, so it could be worth a try to use them while outside Oz.

In the first edition of this book, I also talked about a program that TAW was offering, which guaranteed a job after completing the course. Unfortunately, that guaranteed job offer is no longer available. But I can't help but mention the course because I still think it sounds amazing.

The program is called TAW's Outback Ranch Training. You get a week worth of training, and then granted access to a list of available job contacts upon successful completion of the course.

Basically, you are getting trained to be a cowboy. How awesome is that!

Check out more information on the program here: taw.com.au/Training/OutbackRanchTraining
- Google *Taw outback ranch training*

TAW as a job search engine

The other benefit of TAW is that their website has tons of job listings. What separates them from the pack is that their jobs are legit, no scams. I found my second job, at an outback roadhouse, quite easily through them in a matter of days.

TAW does charge a fee, so if you don't want to use them there is also gumtree.com.au. I used this site sparingly (never with success) but generally used TAW because I didn't want to deal with the potential scams that could happen on gumtree.

Again, don't just search for work online. Tell others what you're looking for, and you may just find it.

Did I get lucky finding high paying gigs?

It's easy to say this, but the reason I chose to go to Australia in the first place was because of the money. During my first three months of backpacking in 2010 and 11, I met over a half dozen travelers who all made a small fortune in Australia. After hearing this enough, I was convinced I could do it too and bought my Work and Holiday visa while in Kuala Lumpur.

Also, I had not one, but two high paying jobs while in Australia. Although the second one I hated and left early.

The point is the high paying jobs are out there if you're willing to make money your priority and loosen your expectations for jobs, locations, and hours.

With Australia's minimum wage at $18 an hour, finding these high paying jobs is still possible, especially if you get out of the city, and into the outback or bush (rural areas) where the cost of living is substantially lower.

A good deal of jobs in the outback or bush will even pay for your accommodation, and potentially your meals. That means every dollar you make, you can stash away for your next travel adventure.

To see what's possible, check out this list of typical Work and Holiday pay rates in Australia: taw.com.au/money/pay-rates
- Google *Taw Australia pay rates*

Conclusion

Where to go from here

If you don't know where you're going, you'll never get there.

So figure out where you want to travel first. Once you do that, start thinking about how you're going to get there, how you'll save up the money, and set a date for when you plan to arrive.

I won't lie; saving up to travel abroad on a small income (especially in your 20's) is not easy.

If I had to start over again, I honestly probably wouldn't do it because of the tremendous effort and focus it took. Yet, the reward of my first 11-month trip abroad was truly amazing. One of the best times in my life easily, and a huge growth experience for me personally.

My second time around when I moved here to Bangkok was much easier. Then I knew what I was doing and challenged myself less by asking for help and moving in with my parents.

The value of travel experience

My first day in Indonesia back in 2010, I awoke at my hostel and met a young, 18 year-old American. He'd been traveling for 11 months starting in

Europe, through the Middle East overland, and was now in SE Asia.

For someone so young, I was impressed by the length of his trip and asked him how he funded it. It was his parent's high school graduation gift, he told me. They gave him a choice of college or money for an extended trip abroad. He chose the latter.

There is a reason why a parent would offer a choice like this, and it's the same reason so many people travel and come back a changed person. When you're traveling, your head isn't stuck in a book contemplating theories and learning from words. Instead, you are gaining valuable hands on life experience.

I previously worked in the US television industry. And when I was starting out, internships were a necessity to get a job. No one cared that I had a degree in Film and Cinematography; they wanted to see experience because what you learned physically on a TV set was intangible and something you could never learn in a classroom. The same goes for travel.

Travel can be intense, and the longer you go the more you learn about yourself, life, and the world outside your borders. Traveling will teach you things you'll never ever learn in your home country or a book.

Thank you

Thank you so much for reading this guide, and I wish you the best in your future travels.

Happy trails, and maybe I'll see you somewhere on the road.

BONUS CHAPTER:

#1 tactic I've used to score 3 jobs abroad

I touched on how to find work abroad in the Australia chapter. In this bonus chapter, I want to dig a little deeper into the most effective ways to find work overseas, specifically focusing on one tactic— the one I used to land 3 out of the 6 jobs I've had overseas.

But before we get to this, what are some of the most common ways to find work overseas?

Teaching English - an easy way to find work

This is one of the most obvious ones. And I invite you to skip this section if you have no interest in teaching English abroad. But for those who want a general understanding of teaching English overseas, read on.

In Thailand, and from what I've heard in other countries, landing teaching work is incredibly easy.

When I first came to Bangkok, I was a teacher. And I easily got four different teaching job offers within my first month here.

Did I enjoy teaching?

It was fun for the year I taught. It gave me a unique look at the inner workings of a third world country's schooling system, which is far different from the US.

With that said, a year of teaching was enough for me. Some people love it though. And after they get one English teaching job, they end up doing it for the rest of their lives.

Depending on where you're teaching, the salary can vary tremendously. In places like South Korea and Dubai, you can make a fortune. In Thailand and other SE Asian countries, it's not that great. You'll earn enough to live comfortably and save a bit of money if you're smart. But you likely won't become rich as a SE Asian English teacher.

How do you find work?

It's pretty simple. You can literally just walk into the local Language schools and inquire about work. You can also find work on online job sites and gain tips from popular teaching English sites. Here's a few below:

- Thailand's premier English teaching site: ajarn.com
- A popular site for aspiring English teachers: eslcafe.com
- The famous English teaching training organization's site: tefl.com

Job boards – many countries have em'

Another obvious one, so I'll keep this short...as I mentioned in the Australia chapter, gumtree.com is a popular job board in Australia. But job boards exist in other countries as well.

While Thailand doesn't have anything like gumtree, they do have a craigslist, as do many countries. So it may be worth exploring these.

Just remember my note from the Australia chapter...when applying for work on job boards, beware that some of them may be scams. If you can find a site that only posts legitimate jobs like TAW, (also mentioned in the Australia chapter) I'd recommend investing the few extra dollars in it to ensure you don't get scammed.

Cruise ship jobs – great way to stockpile money and see the world

This is perhaps one you haven't heard of. But years ago I met a guy in Bangkok who lived and worked aboard cruise ships for 7 years. What I found most fascinating was how much money he saved. As the cruise lines he worked for covered accommodation and food expenses, plus salary, he regularly saved several thousand US dollars a month.

I will straight up say, I am no expert in working aboard cruise lines. I've never done it. But if I went back in time to 2010 when I was planning my first trip abroad, this is something I would've considered.

So if you're interested in this line of work and the potential to cruise the world while saving a ton of cash, I'd recommend exploring cruise jobs.

You're likely to find a wealth of information on Google. And if you can find someone who's lived the cruise life, he or she is sure to be a great resource.

The #1 most effective way to land jobs

Out of the six jobs I've had abroad, I've acquired half through networking. And several more have been offered to me while attending networking events.

If you're considering working abroad, I want to stress the value of attending networking events and talking with as many travelers, locals and people as possible.

Whether you're in Australia, Thailand, South Africa or anywhere in the world, this can make it much easier to land work—especially if you don't want to be an English Teacher! Not that there's anything wrong with teaching, but it's not for everyone. And many travelers prefer a different type of work.

But networking is freaking scary

If you're new to networking, it can be intimidating to talk with strangers. So understand this—everyone is in the same boat as you.

Everyone at networking events is there to meet other people. And travelers and expats are some of the friendliest bunch around.

Out of the thousand or so people I've met while networking, no one has ever once been rude when I've walked up and said, "Hi, my name is John. Do you mind if I join you guys?"

Why networking is effective for winning work

Meeting people face-to-face helps establish trust quickly. So if you attend a networking event and just act genuine (aka be yourself) people will start to trust you.

If you are attending business networking events, you will often meet directly with business owners, or decision makers.

What does this mean for you?

Basically, you are getting a job interview right there on the spot. You don't have to waste time filling out an application, searching through endless job ads online, or going through several interviews before meeting the business owner. Instead, he's right there in front of you. And if he likes you, well, you have a chance of him offering you work, or referring you to a friend who may be searching for employees. Which brings me to the next point...

Referrals. Even if the person you're speaking with isn't the decision-maker, he or she may know decision makers. With the trust you establish by acting like a genuine dude, there's a strong chance that person will refer you to their friends, business owners or other people who may be looking for employees.

Hell, over the years I've referred dozens of people I've met at networking events. And some of them have even scored a job from my referral!

So how can you win with networking?

Talk to as many people as possible – I always aim to talk with around a dozen people within a 2-3 hour networking event. When you're at the event, look to talk with other people who are standing alone, or groups of three or more.

Why avoid two person groups?

Because when just two people are talking, generally they are in a deep discussion. If you go introduce yourself during this discussion, you'll likely interrupt them, which can rub some folks the wrong way.

On the other hand, people by themselves are easy to approach and are usually happy to strike up a chat. And groups of three or more often are incredibly welcoming to more people joining their convo.

Your goal is to make friends – at a networking event, you can tell when people are simply out to score business. They'll hand you a business card immediately, give you a sales pitch, and then get out of there. It's annoying. And out of the many people I've helped at events, it's never these folks. Their business card goes right in the trash.

Instead, just try and make friends. Why? Because people want to help their friends.

Some of my best friends in Bangkok are people I've met at networking events. And to this day we still refer each other work. So, instead of acting desperate for a job, simply try and get to know the other person. Ask where they're from, what they do, how long they've been in the city, etc…

Tell your new friends you're looking for work – making friends doesn't mean you don't tell them you're looking for a job. I highly recommend mentioning exactly what type of work you're after. But instead of just blurting it out awkwardly, let it come naturally.

If you start the conversation being friendly and asking questions, your turn will come. They'll eventually ask you, "What do you do for work?" or "What are you doing in the city?"

This is your time to shine. Simply tell them, "I'm thinking about staying here more permanently, so I'm looking for a job."

Most people naturally want to help others. So the other person will almost undoubtedly ask about what you do, and what kind of work you're looking for.

Of course, not everyone you speak with is going to offer you a job, refer you, or provide a lead. But, if you go to enough events and talk with enough people, it's only a matter of time before you land work.

What events should you attend?

- meetup.com - great place to find events where you can meet travelers and locals. I scored a freelancing gig at a meetup and have been offered a few jobs while attending these events.
- **Chamber of Commerce events** – if you're looking for a higher paying gig, these are typically where the money is. Look up the local chambers—Australian, American, British, etc.—find their events page and see when their next event is.

- **Your hostel's get-togethers** – be aware of the times when fellow travelers are hanging out in the hostel. This could be a happy hour, dinnertime, or an official event the hostel is hosting. These are great times to talk with other travelers about their work experience in the country. And just like my story with Bjorn, you may even get tipped off to a job lead.

I hope you've found this bonus chapter helpful. Again, I know networking is scary if you've never done it before. But, just remember, people at events are there to meet other people. Once you've done a bit of networking, it will get easier. As the saying goes, practice makes perfect.

So good luck with your job hunt overseas. And if you're in Bangkok and looking for work, drop me a line at john@ordinarydudemeditation.com. I can point you to the city's best networking events, and I may just know someone who can help you land a job.

About the author

That's me in 2010. With some local kids in the small Indonesian town of Pangandaran, 3 months into my epic 11-month backpacking trip.

I've been a writer for nearly ten years now, starting off as a scriptwriter in the wonderful world of reality TV, for shows such as National Geographic's *Alaska State Troopers* and the Bio Channel's *Biography Series*. Today, I'm a full time writer for a digital marketing company and run a meditation business on the side at www.ordinarydudemeditation.com.

Originally from Chicago, Illinois, I've now lived in Bangkok for 4+ years. Outside of travel, I'm also a huge fan of NBA bball and a hardcore meditator—meditating for over 15 years now.

Also by the author

Written by an ordinary dude, for ordinary dudes, *An Ordinary Dude's Guide to Meditation* will unravel the perplexing rhetoric often associated with meditation, and speak to you straight.

Packed with **practical explanations** of meditation's **transformational powe**r and step-by-step **instructions on how to meditate**, *An Ordinary Dude's Guide to Meditation* is your first step to gain all the calm and clarity meditation has to offer.

Available at Amazon.com

46306782R00045

Made in the USA
Middletown, DE
26 May 2019